Reverses

REVERSES

Verso works on paper
from the V&A collection

THE COLLECTION
George Eksts

Since 2007 I've worked as a photographer at the V&A in South Kensington, digitising our collection of prints, drawings, paintings and photographs. One day I turned over a Francis Frith landscape photograph (Verso 68) and discovered strange childish drawings on the reverse, then started to notice more marks on the backs of some of the objects I was photographing. Most of our objects have some kind of information on the reverse—usually numbers to identify and locate them within the archive—but I was particularly interested in the accidental marks, damage, fragments of sketches, notes, remnants of reuse, and imprints caused by proximity to other objects that had been stored together. I saw them as unintentional artworks in their own right and, without any thought of a future project, but knowing instinctively that they were worth something, began to photograph them and store the images.

Reverses have their natural habitats. They proliferate among undervalued objects—sketches, unfinished works, scraps of paper. They prefer the older objects—a reflection of the changing value of paper itself. When it was more expensive and harder to come by, it was filled with as much as it could meaningfully hold, and often repurposed. Relative to the artwork, this happened in both directions—drawings were made on the backs of maps or advertisements; shopping and to-do lists were written on the backs of drawings. It's always a pleasure to see everyday life intruding into the hermetic world of art. Verso 150 has a list of expenses including bread, wine and firewood, which gives a wonderfully visual and very relatable glimpse into the life of an artist in the 16th century. Another favourite just says 'RON' inside a heart (Verso 51).

Hierarchies are glimpsed, then inverted—designs and sketches generally have more on the reverse, finished fine artworks have less. Similarly in terms of scale, small objects tend to hold more than larger ones. The average object in this collection is probably about the size of a paperback novel.

As the project gained momentum, I began to open boxes of objects for photography with one thought in mind—would there be any good reverses within? I hoped to see an unruly mess of old envelopes (many with the HMSO imprint to remind me of the clerical nature of my actual work) and improvised paper folders with beautifully scrawled pencil text, out of which a jumble of unmounted sketches or prints might spill. My heart would sink on seeing an orderly stack of card window mounts, each holding an individual artwork in a one-dimensional prison cell.

Although card mounts were my enemy, objects that had once been mounted and later removed might bear blobby marks of glue and torn paper that documented their travels like a stamped passport, revealing their early lives before accession into the museum and its modern conservation practices. Pictures were ruthlessly cut in half, the knife wielder's attention on the recto, leaving only the neck of a vase or the southern half of Ireland. Less arbitrarily, other reverses showed a direct relationship with the recto—the hand-painted back panels of a stereograph meant to tint the light passing through its translucent paper, or the blue crayon rubbed all over the verso to transfer the image to a third surface.

None of these objects are on permanent display—they're kept in boxes stored in locked cabinets within locked rooms. However, anybody can visit the Prints & Drawings Study Room and request to see these and any other objects in the collection. I consider it a great privilege to have been able to spend thousands of hours photographing the archives, and to bring these hidden treasures to light. This is a work in progress—I still have an almost endless supply of objects to photograph, and will hopefully find many more surprising reverses, even more wonderful than the 'official' collection at the Museum.

VERSOS

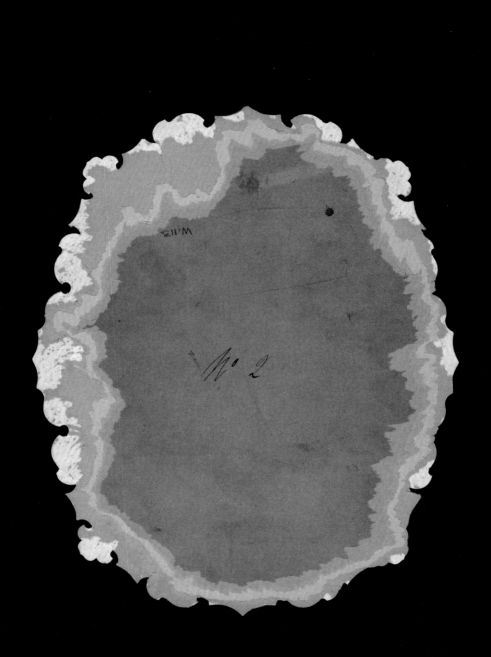

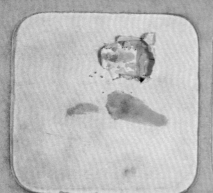

Anthony (UK)

E1966-1099

3436-276

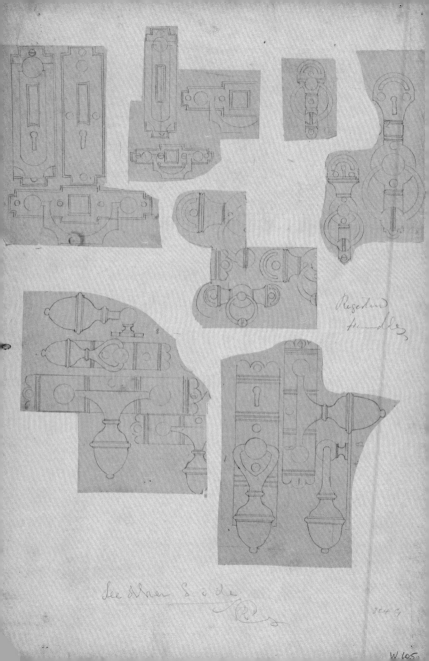

Regular
Handles

See other side
Reg

W.105.

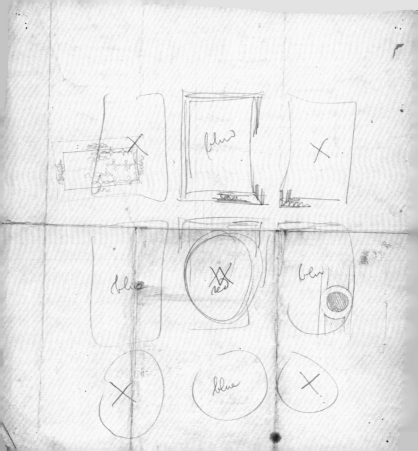

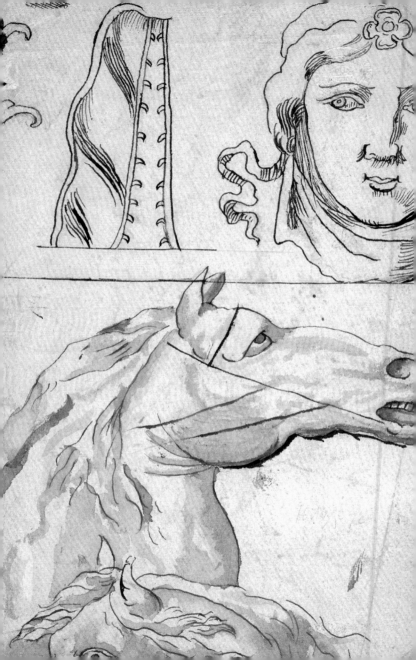

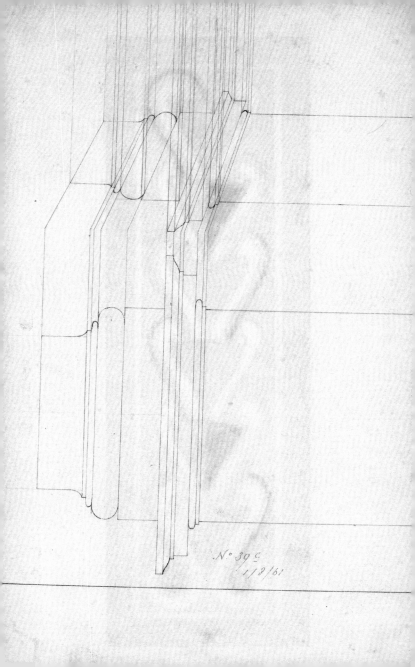

N.° 39 c
118/61

Money
Passport
Drawing and Painting Mat. Sketch Book
3 Things / Great Coat Portmanteau
Truth and Italian Books
Cognari — Hoppenar —
    Address Padua
Letter —
Scagliali li Tavolo
Cocademia
        12 "

        35
        35
        20
        9

        9 2

Silver Paper
Money
Switzer and Aroff
Capel

Money
Passport
Painting Mat.
Chalks &c
Sketch Book
Books Truth and Italian
Address Padua
Tagliali
Academia
Cognaris

P.D. 180°

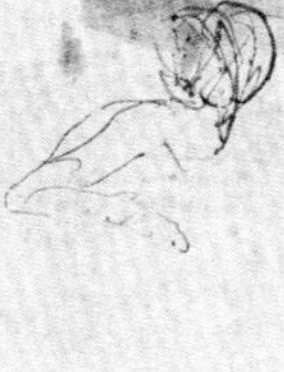

PD. 180ᶜ

LONDON INSTITUTION.

NOVEMBER, 1845.

The COMMITTEE *of* MANAGEMENT *of this* INSTITUTION, *having had frequent representations of the inconvenience of the Admission to the Lectures by the production of the Medals, have this year resolved on attempting a change in the arrangement.* They, *therefore,* enclose *a* CARD OF ADMISSION, to be used by the Nominees of the Proprietors, instead of the Bronze Medals, which will no longer admit to the Lectures.

Each Proprietor is requested to write his Name and Address on the back of the Card ; but the Proprietors themselves, as heretofore, will not be required to produce either Card or Medal.

WILLIAM TITE,
Hon. Sec.

N.B. *Those Proprietors who possess the Additional* BRASS MEDALS, *are requested to apply to* Mr. THOMSON, *at the* LONDON INSTITUTION, between the hours of Two and Three o'clock, who, upon the production of those Medals, *is authorised to issue Tickets in respect thereof.*

P.D. 1808.

Stewarts
Monkey
~~crossed out~~
Thomson
Le Jeun
Butterworth
Moore
Evans
Blanche

Miss E. Lefevre

Hounslow

Middlesex

Choicée

②

John Upton

77

Small
French Ring

694313
Sandra

E. 1821-1977

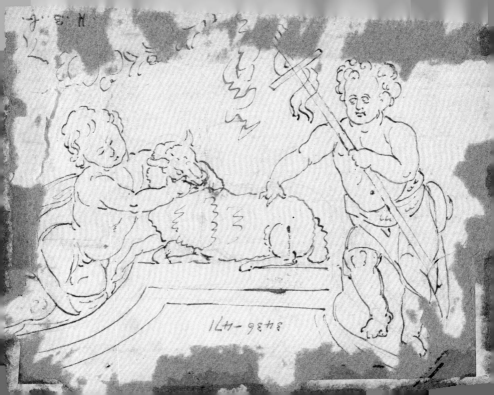

Academy knaves

British Gallery

Camden House =

Chelsea

(☺) Barings Head =

Mrs Stewart

– Soho Square Road

Pearson —

Ramsay —

Daguerrotype

Duke Street

Print Champney

Stewart

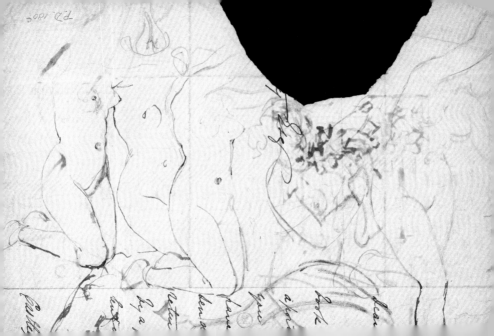

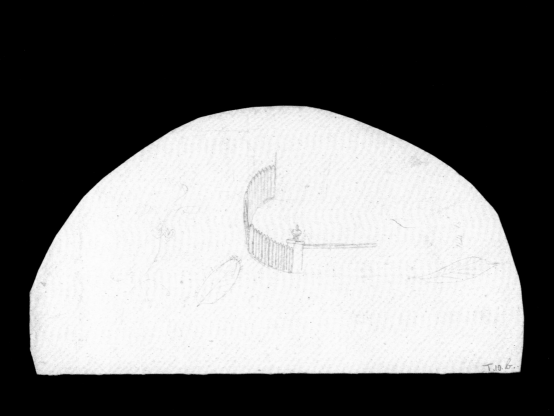

21

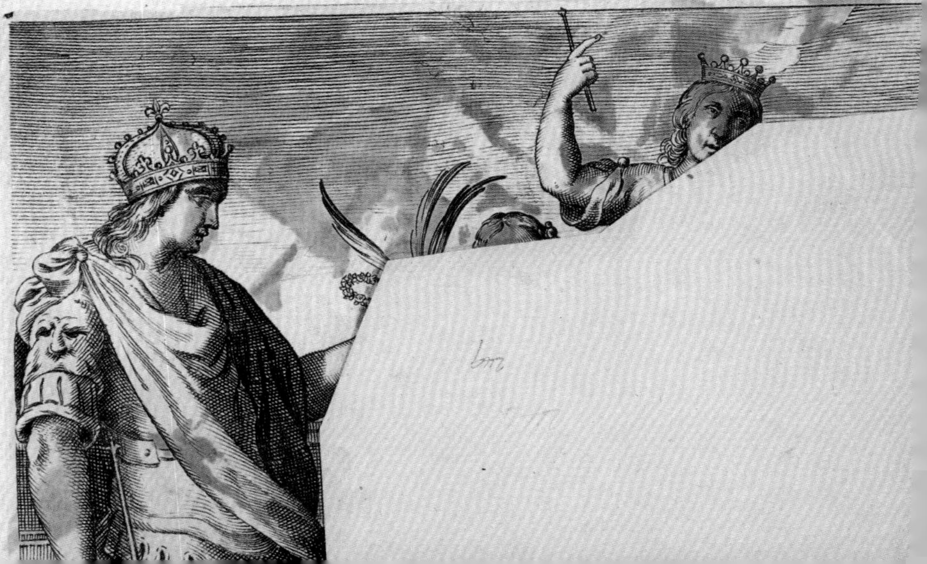

III

8952
53

W102a

all well that ends well — Act 4 Sc 3

gul. 19

PD 207

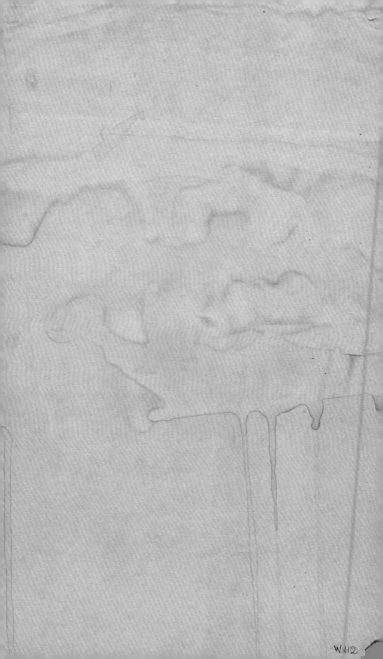

W.112

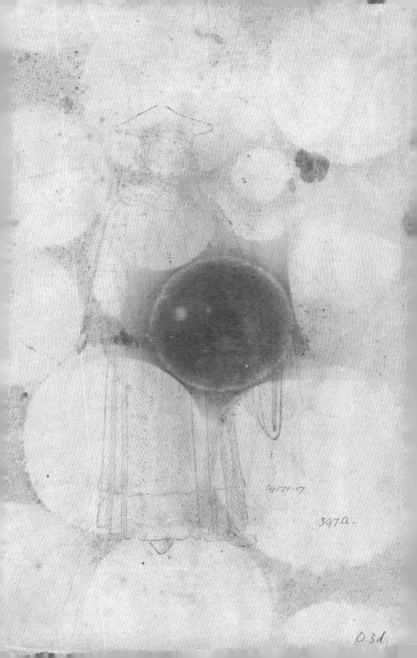

29090.07

397.a.

D.3d.

397.a.

O.3d

Commercial Rd Lambeth

Jany 13th 1843

Sir

I beg you will receive this as a small acknowledgement for your kindness in giving your recommendation letter to the Royal Academy I have to say I am admitted as a Probationary and I trust if I am admitted as a Student I shall not prove unworthy of your kindness and of the Professor

I remain Sir your very humble Servant Charles J S Kelsey

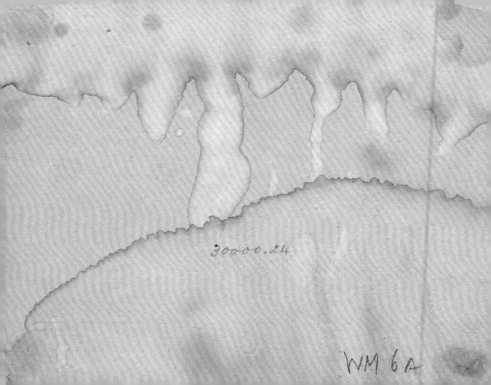

30000.24

WM 6A

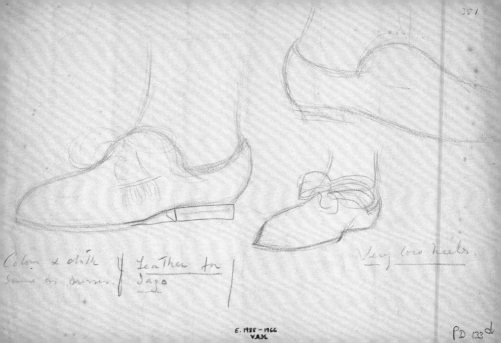

Colour & cloth
Same as ourses.

Leather for
Jago

Very low heels.

N° 578
Naudet Md d'estampes au Louvre 1792
Reverdino
B. XV p. 485 no 35
18/12 57

2h 007. 1.

WM 6A

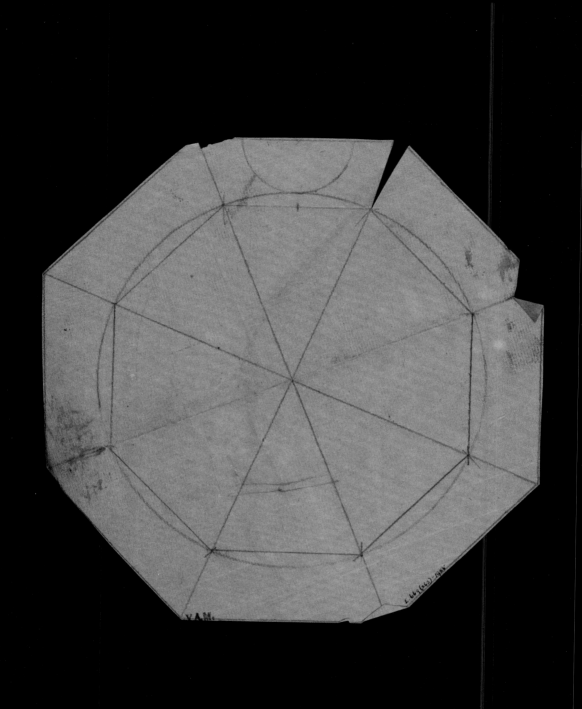

Austin   Fecit -   7-6.

V. A. M

E. 214-1919.

s finished, the remai—
a the urn. This part of the ceremony v
of the Latins.

last sepulchres we opened differed in some
d proved to be of the highest palæograph
ng taken off the cover, we found three larg
ver the tomb, with the convex side upwa
ooved together in an ingenious manner.
as a hole made for and adapted to the for
l them on the tomb. Each of these pe
a thin sheet of lead to prevent the ea
omb only contained a fine dust; probabl
r there were very few remains of bones;
d into powder.

29486
100

9955-8.

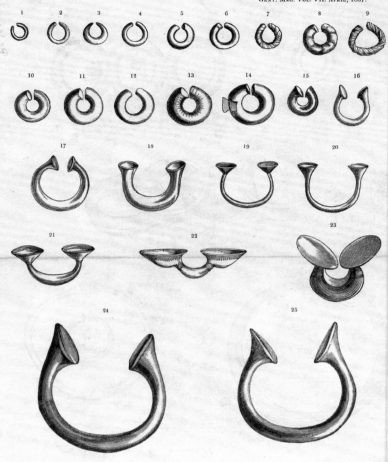

RING-MONEY, OR MANILLAS.

Nos. 1—13, 15—23, are of Gold, and found in Ireland.　　No. 14.—Of Brass, plated with Gold.
No. 24.—An ancient Brass or Bronze Manilla, found in Monaghan.
No. 25.—Manilla, fabricated in England, and now passing current in Africa.

WM 2A

Fig. 31

DOMINVS · LEGEM
DAT·VALERIO SEVERO
EVTROPI VIVAS

25016. 700

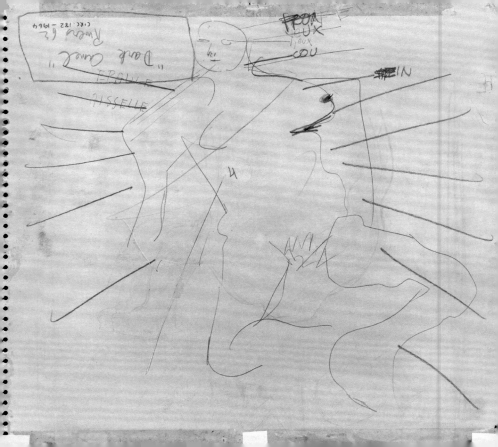

CIRC. 182 – 1964
Pierre 62
"Dark Curve"
FRONT
YEUX
COU
SEIN

FRONT
PISSELLE

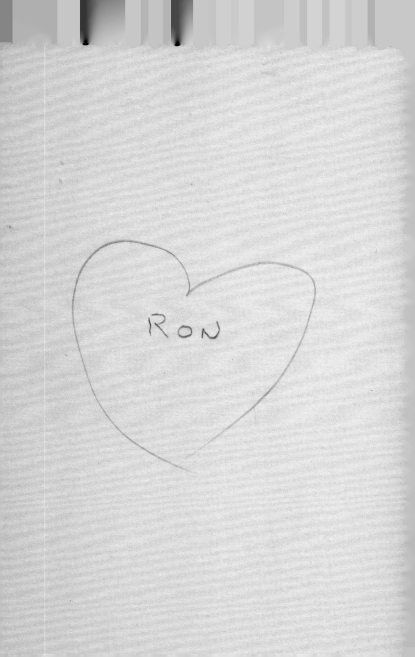

Henry Moore
about 1936
HM

4746

hh

D. 103. '85

15

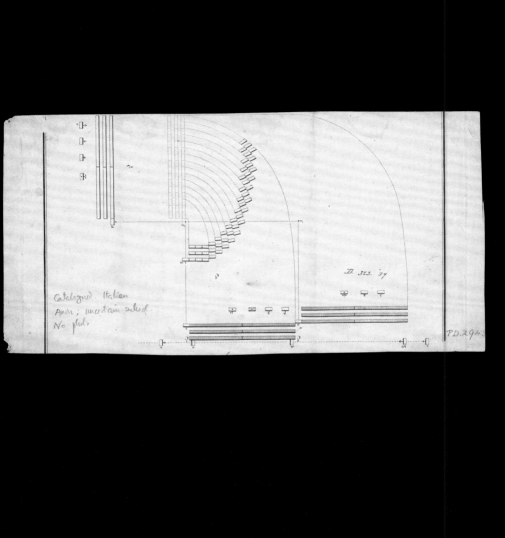

Catalogued: Italian
Anon; uncertain school.
No plate.

D. 323. 37

PD.294.

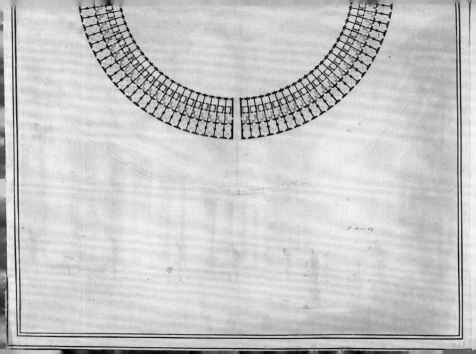

pour la ... fo main 1440
dupuis ayelez
3 beuf a 140 ... pies 510
4 beuf a 22 ... pies 900
        1410

pour la 6 ... main 1440
dupuis
2 ... a ... pies 350
... a 10 pies 810
... mouton a 22 ... pies
        1286

pour la ... fo main 1440
dupuis ayelez
4 beuf a 140 ... pies 750 ... Melegran
1 mouton a 13 pies 151 ...
1 mouton a ... 119 ...
        810 ... 1120

pour la ... fo main
dupuis a jelez

2 mouton a 13 ... pies 162
dupuis a jeter
4 beuf a 10 pies — 850 ...
4 pour St. legraus
a 10 ... 10 pies 632

pour la ... fo main ...
dupuis ayelez
30 mouton a 9 ... pies 249 ...

Dalton Bequest, 1900.
D-1680-1900

14

... 4 beuf a 19 ... pies 1100
2 beuf a 193 ... 836
        2657

pour la 12 ... main 1440
4 beuf a 200 ... pies 1400

pour la 13 fo mein 1440
6 beuf 204 ... 10 — 1245
2 beuf 218 ... — 430
13 mouton a 13 ... pies 169
4 mouton 18 ... pies 126
        1970

ou les pere ... est dus ... et
dieu nous donne un bonne ...
1471
du mardi a go les la pro ...
11 beuf a 240 ... pies 960
3 beuf a 200 ... pies 740
13 mouton a 22 ... pies 286
2 mouton a 36 ... — 108
4 mouton a 30 ... pies 182
        2376

pour la ... fo main 1471
dupuis ayelez

Ramage

V.A.M.

W.102

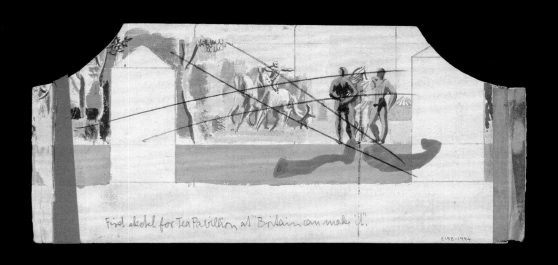

First sketch for Tea Pavillion at "Britain can make it".

E158-1994

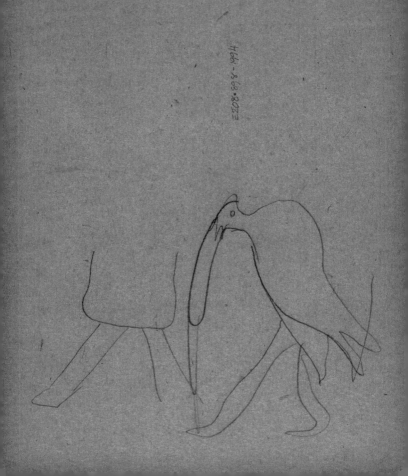

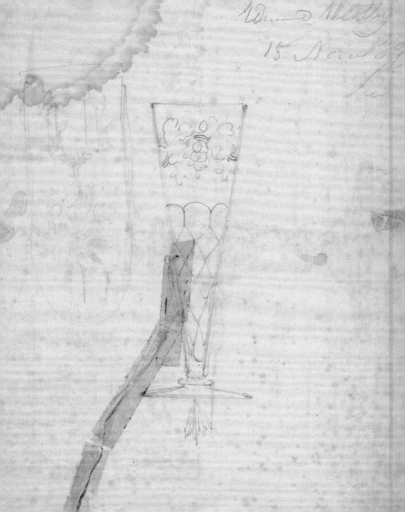

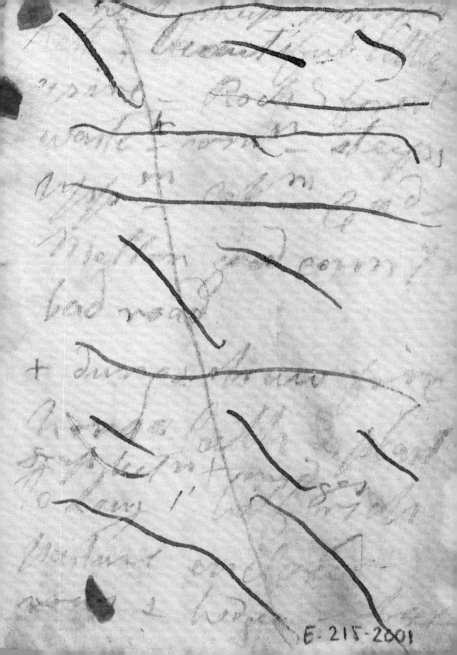

E·215·2001

V. A. M.

E. 231-1924
V. A. M.

richest and most elaborate spe[...] whole extent of the ruins. Ori[...] painted, the marks of red colo[...] distinctly visible. The s[...] of this figure are very sir[...] be no general arrangem[...] or d[...] ornament appears as if placed [...] sculptor without any other inten[...] of filling up a space.

The three large engravings on [...] page are from three of the fou[...] altar, which, says Mr. Stephens, [...] curious a subject of speculation [...] ment in Copan. The altars, like [...] all monolithic, or of a single block [...] general they are not so richly or[...] are more faded and worn, or cove[...] some were completely buried, an[...] was difficult to make out more t[...] * * * This stands on four glo[...] the same stone; the sculpture i[...] and it is the only specimen of that [...] ture found at Copan, all the rest [...] alto-relievo. It is six feet square [...] high, and the top is divided into th[...] of hieroglyphics, which beyond [...] some event in the history of th[...] people who once inhabited the cit[...]

At Gueguetenago were found tw[...] vases here introduced; two of t[...] humed by Mr. Stephens and his co[...] a mound; the tripod was discove[...] Allowing for peculiarity of orna[...] accustomed to Greek and Roman d[...] are not unworthy of being rank[...] works of industrial Art.

We have left ourselves but l[...] comment on the volume before u[...] of interesting travel, and can onl[...] that it is both amusing and instr[...] in an exceedingly pleasant and un[...] qualities to ensure wide popula[...] the book demands and must secu[...] dents of the journey in [...]om[...] known and half-civilised country a[...] mixed up with the antiquarian res[...] enterprising travellers.

ve rather than his descriptive | powers—we extract his remarks on the ruins.

on the very edge of the wall, and | we were surrounded. Who were the people that penetrate the mystery by which | built this city? In the ruined cities of Egypt,

as diftw
of the Attempt, "Can the King. to
morrow kill me; there is no P
angerous than this. This
vell as Estates, which they wou
A certain Prince of *Tartary* usually
n which was engraven the Head of
o in invading his Kingdom loft his
but the edge of which was this Infcr

WM SB

s Prince by coveting mine, loft his own
E 254—'97

e same thing befell King *Sancho*,
s Brothers of the Kingdoms, whic
dinand had divided between 'em
en it but puts its Arm out of its
which runs a Rifque whenever it
nd though *Tyridates* faid, That
naintain their own, but for King
t this is only then, when reaf an

E 1154 '85

? van Vliet

"I will change my nationality
willingly to be a British subject
to Italian," he said. "I have
been in and out of prison these
last three years, month after
month."

Tornelli was found guilty of
breaking a plate-glass window
worth £15 in a hardware store
in Lambs Conduit-street, Hol-
born, and was remanded in cus-
tody for a medical and mental
report.

Father Feared Child Had Polio

Leslie Lee Quidick, 40, of
Hillingdon-road, Gravesend,
who was killed by a train at
Sole, has Tuberstation, was
"much worried" because he
thought his youngest child had
polio, it was stated at a St Pan-
cras inquest today.

A doctor had told him that the
child might be sickening for
measles.

Verdict: Suicide while of
unsound mind.

At Work Again

The Allied Security Board has
told the Deutsche Werke A. G.
Company of Kiel, which built
battleships for Hitler, that they
can again build commercial
ships, says AP.

2-Year Job

Special football services
operate from midday on lines
serving Wembley.

These include the Bakerloo
and Metropolitan lines to Wembley Park. Piccadilly to Alper-
ton. Euston to Wembley (Central) and a special 10-minute
service of steam trains from
Marylebone direct to Wembley
Stadium station which is being
specially opened

Extra Buses

Bus and trolley-bus services
will be strengthened before and
after the game.

More than 200 police will be
on duty. Walkie-talkies will
will be used to control the
100,000 crowd and thousands of
cars and coaches going to the
match.

Gates are to be opened
shortly after midday. In addi-
tion to community singing the
band of the Royal Marines
(Deal) will entertain the crowd
for an hour before the kick-off.

Of the 73 games played between the two countries. Scotland have won 32 and England
23. At the last Wembley game
in 1951 the Scots won 3—

Knot Suitable

Bow ties were made compul-
sory for assistants at a big
meat establishment near Wel-
lington, New Zealand, after the
proprietor had found that loose
ties were being caught in

E 425 -1967

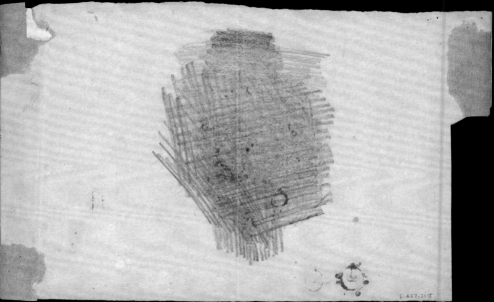

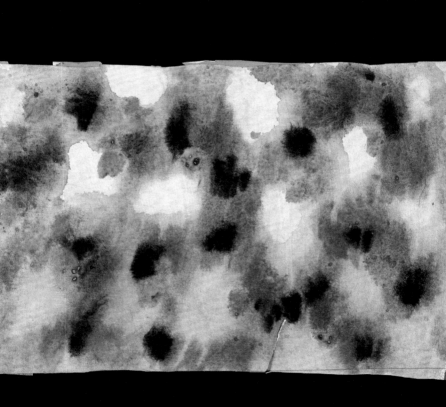

9. 5. 1950.

...und viele herzliche Grüße und
Küsse an dich liebe Lily,
Hermann, Bub001 und
Ruth von deiner dich liebenden
Mutter.

Überbringe der Mutter beste Grüße.

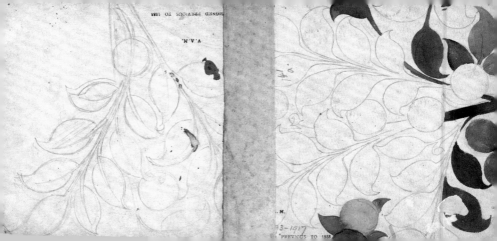

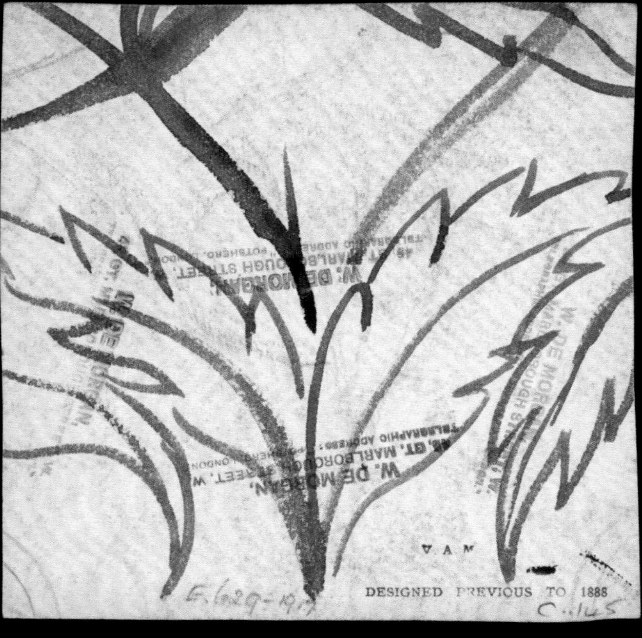
E.629-1917
DESIGNED PREVIOUS TO 1888
C.145

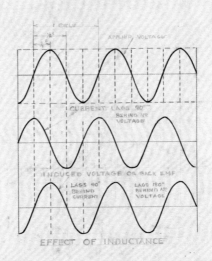

EFFECT OF INDUCTANCE

E.2081-1966.
V.A.M.

PD.133d

E 2016-1966

V.A.M. E 2016-1966   PD. 133d

DESIGNED PREVIOUS TO 1888

C. 145

E, 840 - 1987

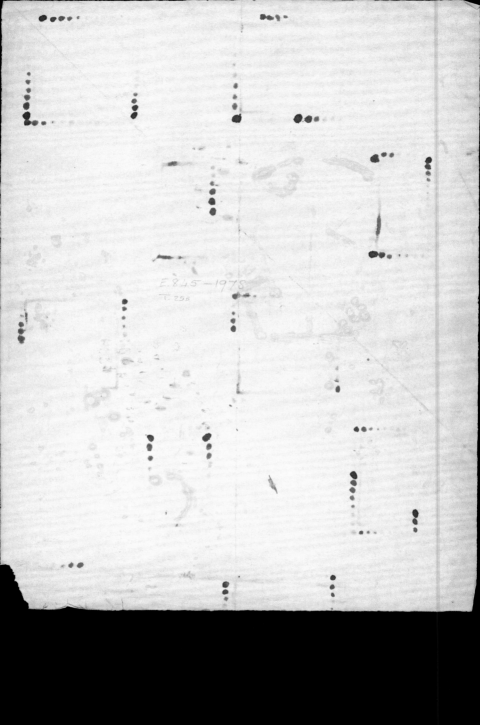

E.845—1978
T.258

DESIGNED PREVIOUS TO 1888

V. A. M.

E. 906-1917

C 145

GG 72(c)

V.A.M.

E.958-1917

C 145

E. 948 - 1921.

VAM

E. 978 - 1921

W. 102

E. 1259. 117 - 86

WM 3c

W. 3. c.

savages; but savages never reared
savages never carved the[...] stones.
Indians who made the[...] and th[...]
was 'Quien sabe?' '[...]

"There were no a[...] [...]
place; none of those stirr[...] rec[...]
hallowed Rome, Athens, and [...]

'The world's great mistress on the [...]

but architecture, sculpture, and [...]
Arts which embellished life, had f[...]
overgrown forest; orators, warrior[...]
beauty, ambition, and glory, had [...]
away, and none knew that such th[...]
or could tell of their past existen[...]
record of knowledge, are silent[...]
The city was desolate. No remn[...]
hangs around the ruins, with tra[...]
down from father to son, and fro[...]
generation. It lay before us like a[...]
in the midst of the ocean, her mast[...]
effaced, her crew perished, and non[...]
she came, to whom she belonged, [...]
voyage, or what caused her destr[...]
people to be traced only by some [...]
blance in the construction of the [...]
haps, never to be known at all. T[...]
we sat, was it a citadel from whic[...]
people had sounded the trumpe[...]
temple for the worship of the god o[...]
the inhabitants worship the idols [...]
own hands, and offer sacrifices on t[...]
them? All was mystery—dark, im[...]
tery—and every circumstance in [...]
Egypt the colossal skeletons of g[...]
stand in the unwatered sands in al[...]
of desolation; here an immense [...]
the ruins, hiding them from sight, [...]
impression and moral effect, and gi[...]
and almost wildness to the interest [...]

The large engraving on the [...]
copied from a stone idol [...] opan[...]
feet high, and stands [...] s fa[...]
east; its breadth is f[...] feet, [...]
three feet, sculptured on all fo[...]
from the base to the top, and [...]

FAIRHOLT

THE RESIDENC

...e people of Nuremberg, and th........
...ghbourhood, figure as repr........
...ent Jews. St. Joseph is a N........
...ar... th... Virgin herself .... to ...

E.1284—1917

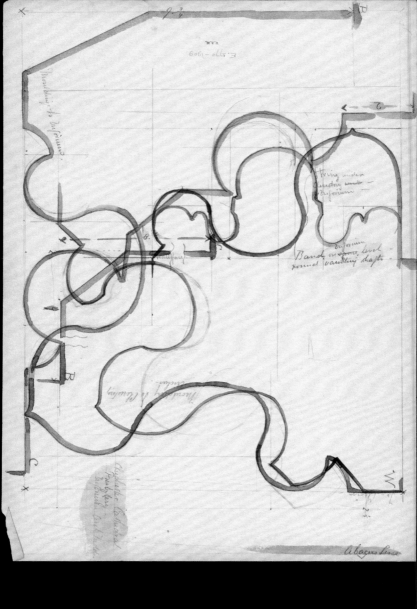

E.1437. 1914

E. 1349 — 1914

738

E 1300-1935
E

E.1500 - 1935

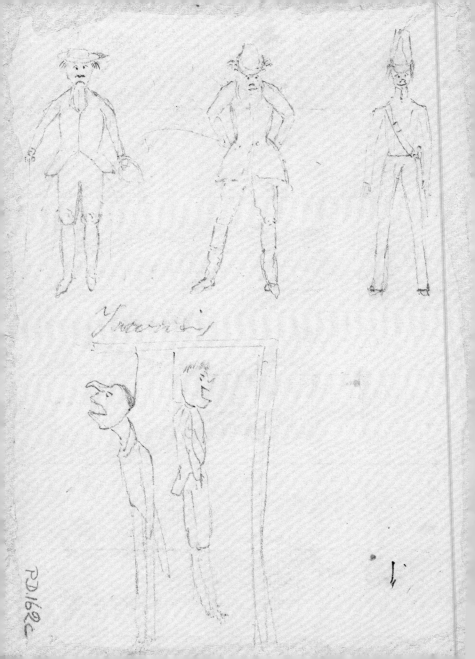

PD.162c

196.

V. A. M.

From

CONTINENTAL
DAILY PARCELS EXPRESS
53, GRACECHURCH STREET.
LONDON, E.C.

Date

From

CONTINENTAL
DAILY PARCELS EXPRESS
53, GRACECHURCH STREET.
LONDON, E.C.

E. 1400—1917

E 1332 -1966

V.A.M.

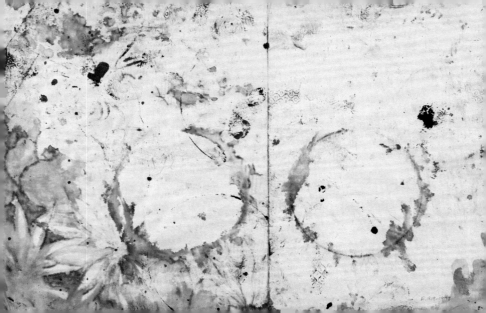

E.1818-1977

E. 152/ A 180 — '85

WM4c

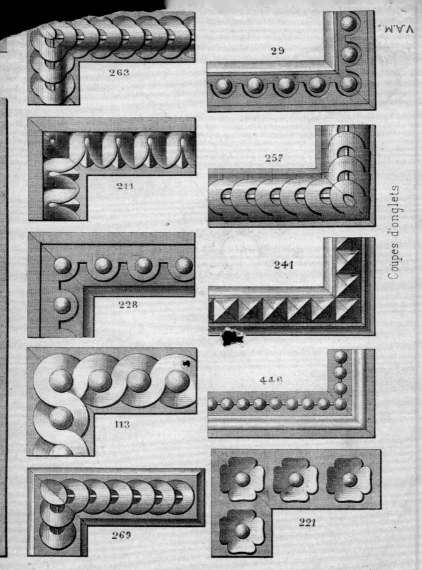

Coupes d'onglets

263

29

211

257

228

241

113

446

269

221

t toute sculpture soupçonnée à l'action de l'eau bouillante.

ANONYMOUS: Furniture & Furnishing
Sheet of designs for chair-back and sash handles, probably manufactured by Cope & Timmins Ltd, ironfounders and factors' merchants, 10 Soho Square, London. Late 19th to early 20th century.
Lithograph with ink, each number, measurements and prices.
Lithograph 8⅛ × 13⅜ (20.8 × 33.4 cm)
Note: These designs formed part of the stock of the firm of E. Lawrence
[cat. E.1924-1969]

E.1924-1966

m.1533-1966

V.A.M.

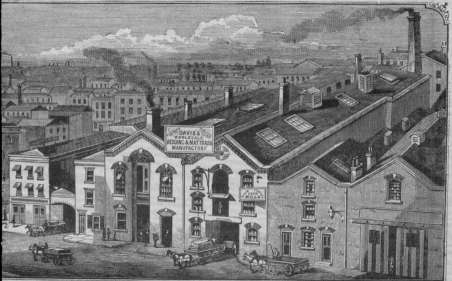

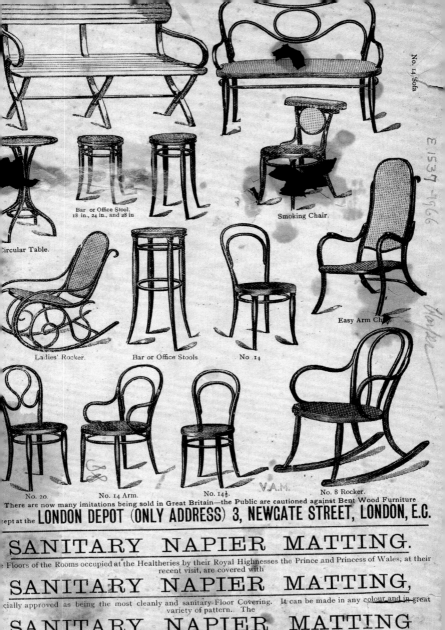

No. 14 Sofa

E.1537-1966

Bar or Office Stool.
18 in., 24 in., and 28 in.

Smoking Chair.

Circular Table.

Easy Arm Chair

Ladies' Rocker.

Bar or Office Stools

No .14

No. 20.

No. 14 Arm.

No. 14½.

V.A.M.

No. 8 Rocker.

There are now many imitations being sold in Great Britain—the Public are cautioned against Bent Wood Furniture ...cept at the **LONDON DEPOT (ONLY ADDRESS) 3, NEWGATE STREET, LONDON, E.C.**

SANITARY NAPIER MATTING.

.. Floors of the Rooms occupied at the Healtheries by their Royal Highnesses the Prince and Princess of Wales, at their recent visit, are covered with

SANITARY NAPIER MATTING,

...cially approved as being the most cleanly and sanitary Floor Covering.   It can be made in any colour and in great variety of pattern.   The

SANITARY NAPIER MATTING

...made entirely BY HAND, and is greatly superior to the many imitations which its success has called into existence.

E.1620-197

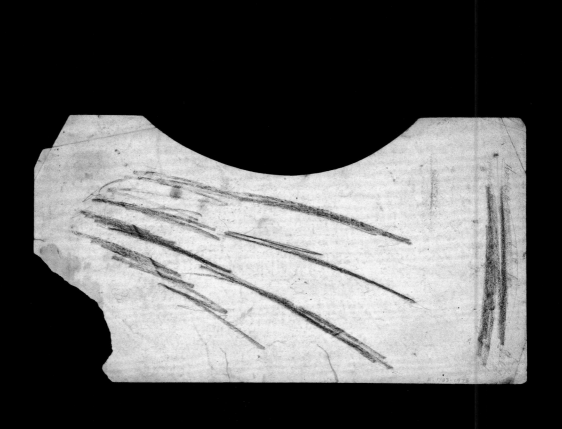

highest references; moderate salary.—"Energetic," office of this journal.

YOUNG MAN, aged 27, with good business abilities, DRAUGHTSMAN AND DESIGNER, is open for situation.—T. B. Hunt, 1a, Rossington Street, Upper Clapton.

A CABINET FOREMAN, experienced; thoroughly practical; understands machinery and preparing working drawings; three years in present situation; excellent reference.—T. N., 73, Westwick Gardens, W.

SALESMAN, BUYER, TRAVELLER, or to Manage a Branch. Wanted by a good all-round man, Situation as above; good Draughtsman; can take measurements, give estimates, &c.—"Rota," office of this journal.

YOUNG MAN desires Situation in good Cabinet Shop, with chance of improvement.—H. G., office of this journal.

SITUATION required by JUNIOR DRAUGHTSMAN; miniature and working drawings.—Address S., office of this journal.

FRENCH POLISHER.—Experienced Man wants work in all branches; good references.—Smithson, 221, Portland Road, Notting Hill.

BUSINESS ADVERTISEMENTS.

ART FRET CUTTING, Moulding, and four-square Cutting done in the best style, and on reasonable terms, by A. C. Cadman, 20, Ironmonger Row, Old Street, London, E.C.

AMERICAN ELM BENT SHAFTS, &c., for Children's Mail Carts, supplied by the Victor Cycle Company, 167, Victor Street, Grimsby.

GOLD and SILVER PLATING, ELECTRO-BRONZING, LACQUERING, NICKEL PLATING, OXIDIZING.— Cabinet Makers, Antique Dealers, &c., should try J. G.

THE PICTORIAL WORLD

An Illustrated Weekly Newspaper,

PRICE THREEPENCE.

Offices:—63, Fleet Street, London,

187

119

E. 1805—1966

E. J. Forbes-Robertson

E. J. Forbes-Robertson

E. J. Forbes-Robertson

My Dear Jane

Sir ——

WVA
E. 1809-1966

Would you oblige me with
a ticket for the forthcoming
lectures at the Academy

I remain your
obedient servant
Forbes-Robertson

Eric not Job

S11

E. 1866. 89

Ceilings.

Q. 13d

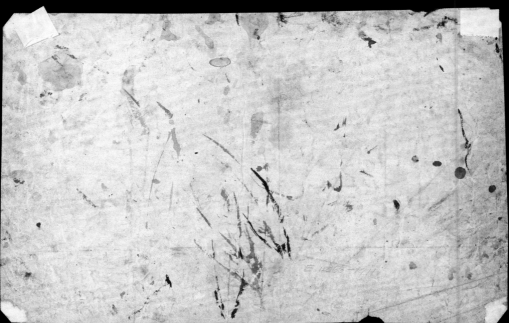

All All Goods SUPPLIE

PD. 133 d

F cara. os

E. Th 81. Th

GOV

POLAND

NEW RUSSIA

LITTLE

Zaporiski Cosaks

ZAPORISKE Cosacks

TARTAR

Nogay Ta

NEWRUSSIA

Lemberg

Poltawa

Kiow

Korsun

Archangelgorod

Kherson

Otchakow

Budzak

Bessarabia

Kilia nova

Ismail

Mouths of the Danube

Akkerman Belgorod

KRIM
now Karasubazar

TAURIDA

Bakczisarai

Sebastopol

Perecop

SEA CE

Bo 221

Gulf of

St Antioco

Isola
Palma

Golfo
di Saria

Budillo

Tonaca

Faro

A Tore

Capo de la Sav

Pietra di Sale

Tora di Figa

Tore di
Cortelazzo

Neola di Pola

Tore Calada bret

Scope d'Ancha
al Tore

Isola dell Gudes

L S. Stefano

12345

(?) Powerscourt, Ireland.
Inscribed Poscourt Ireland.
Pen and ink and wash. (6¾ × 9)   E. 1319–1924.

E. 1319 – 1924
V. A. M.

256

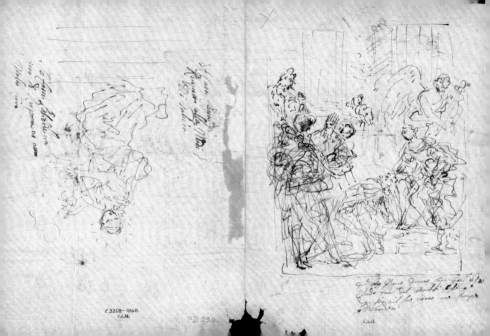

LES LIVRES

1902.

✗ 16

E.1854-1966 V.AM. 166

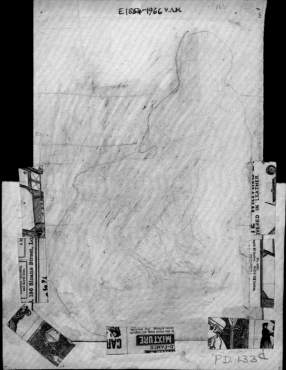

P.D.133d

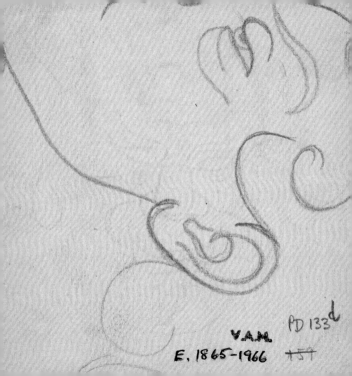

No 46

E. LIYAM 66
E-2103-1966

PD 133d

Vino — ℈ = :60
Pane — " = :18
Vino — " = :24
Pane — " = :12
Legna — " = :27
Totale — ℈ = 141 =

4688

Questo è un Libbro che si Descrive le Sorte

7298

RECTOS

1
HENRY ARCHER
A drawing on paper for a design for an oval mirror. *Oval Mirror with figure of 'Time' and 'Truth'.* England, about 1871.
V&A: 7797

2
UNKNOWN
Specimen with coloured flower motif. Possibly to be used as a picture mount. Gold embossed card.
V&A: 75A/13

3
UNKNOWN
Interieur de Harem, anonymous tissue stereograph with two albumen prints showing a room decorated with tapestries and chandeliers, populated by women and male servants. France, late 19th century.
V&A: 663-1943

4
MARK ANTHONY
Stereoscopic photograph of a gathering of men and women in a grand dining room for the London Stereoscopic Company. Britain, 1850s.
V&A: 1366-1992

5
UNKNOWN
One of 512 architectural drawings and sketches by various architects, artists and designers collected by the architect Charles James Richardson, and bought from him by the Museum in 1863.
V&A: 3436:276

6
R. CHARLES
One of 15 sheets of drawings of various furniture handles. Pencil on paper, mounted on to board. Britain, dated 1875, one being 1871.
V&A: 8118:27

7
ALFRED STEVENS
One of 12 sketches and scraps. Drawing on paper. Britain, about 1850.
V&A: 8597E

8
UNKNOWN
Sketch for ornament with amorino.
V&A: 1101:4

9
LUDWIG GRUNER
A multi-coloured design featuring a triangular motif and bordered in black. One of a series of 16 copies of Italian decoration. Coloured ink on paper. Italy, mid 19th century.
V&A: 1735

10
WILLIAM ETTY
Sheet of sketches of figures and parts of figures. One of 347 studies and scraps of drawing. Pencil on paper. Britain, about 1820–45.
V&A: 7652:14

11
WILLIAM ETTY
Sheet of sketches, including studies of legs. One of 347 studies and scraps of drawing. Pen and ink. Britain, about 1820–45.
V&A: 7650:28

12
WILLIAM ETTY
Study of a horse (1 of 73, that form part of a group of 347 studies and scraps of drawing). Pencil and pen on paper. Britain, about 1820–45.
V&A: 7654:58

13
WILLIAM ETTY
Landscape study. One of 347 sketches and scraps of miscellaneous subjects. Pencil and pen on paper. Britain, about 1820–45.
V&A: 7655:6

14
WILLIAM ETTY
One of 347 sketches and scraps of miscellaneous subjects. Pencil and pen on paper. Britain, about 1820–45.
V&A: 7650:23

15
WILLIAM ETTY
Studies of human anatomy. One of 347 sketches and scraps of miscellaneous subjects. Pencil on paper. Britain, about 1820–45.
V&A: 7653:4

16
JOHN UPTON
A two panel design for a mural known as *'The Secret Island'* for the Milner and King-swood council flats. Showing a psychedelic scene of buildings, planes, flowers, rainbows and flowers. Felt pen on paper. England, about 1975.
V&A: E.1821-1977

17
UNKNOWN
Drawing of three statues: a seated draped woman holding a bird, a man wearing a toga and holding a book, and an older woman with her head covered. This object was once part of an album of designs by various architects, artists and designers collected by the architect Charles James Richardson. Pen and ink drawing on paper. Europe, before 1863.
V&A: 3436:471

18
WILLIAM ETTY
One of 347 sketches and scraps of miscellaneous subjects. Pencil and pen on paper. Britain, about 1820–45.
V&A: 7650:70

19
WILLIAM ETTY
Sketches of nude female figures. One of 347 sketches and scraps of miscellaneous subjects. Pencil and pen on paper. Britain, about 1820–45.
V&A: 7651:36

20
WILLIAM ETTY
Landscape study with a river running through a mountainous valley, with a tall tree in the foreground. Pencil and pen drawing on blue paper. Britain, about 1820–45.
V&A: 7655:10

21
JOSEPH NEIL PATON
Semicircular design for a damask cloth, with flowers, pineapples and an ear of corn. Pen and ink drawing on paper. Scotland, mid 19th century.
V&A: 362:17

22
UNKNOWN
Drawing of a rear view
of a male figure, draped
in a cloth covering one
shoulder, pointing upward
with his left hand. From
a collection of drawings
of human anatomy.
Chalk on paper. Europe,
about 19th century.
V&A: 8640G

23
GIOVANNI BAGLIONE
Drawing of a concert,
with a seated youth,
clothed, playing a lute,
a nude winged youth
playing a tambourine
and four other figures
seated and reclining.
Pen and ink and wash
over black chalk. Italy,
about 1600–44.
V&A: 8641I

24
UNKNOWN
Drawing, furniture and
architectural elevations.
V&A: 8952:55

25
THOMAS STOTHARD
Sketches of groups of
people, including two
sketches of heads.
Pen and ink on paper.
England, about 1815.
V&A: 9241:19

26
M. WIRTH
Design for a fireplace
surround. One of 141
furniture designs on
84 sheets. Printed on
blue paper. Europe,
18th–early 19th century.
V&A: 28394:2

27
UNKNOWN
Print depicting a
full-length male figure
wearing a square cap,
a fur cape over a
voluminous gown and
holding a book in his
left hand. Woodcut on
paper. Germany, early
16th century.
V&A: 29878:17

28
UNKNOWN
Print depicting a
full-length male figure
wearing a brimmed hat
with three feathers, a
collared shirt with tie
at neck, a skirt with a
sword at his waist and
pointed shoes. Woodcut
on paper. Germany,
early 16th century.
V&A: 29878:23

29
JACQUES LE MOYNE
DE MORGUES
Botanical painting of a
twig from the walnut tree,
with both a halved and
a whole walnut. This
drawing belongs to an
album of 59 botanical
watercolours on paper.
France, about 1575.
V&A: AM.3267CC-1856

30
WILLIAM ETTY
One of 347 sketches and
scraps. Pencil and pen
on paper studies of
miscellaneous subjects.
Britain, about 1820–45.
V&A: 7653:7

31
WILLIAM ETTY
One of 347 sketches
and scraps of miscellane-
ous subjects. Pencil and
pen on paper. Britain,
about 1820–45.
V&A: 7653:13

32
STELLA, JACQUES
(artist)
STELLA CLAUDINE
(etcher)
'Le Jeu des Espingles',
etching from the series
'Les Jeux et Plaisirs de
l'Enfance', showing 7
nude children at play.
There are trees in the
background and 6 lines
of French verse along
the bottom. France, 1657.
V&A: 30000:24

33
UNKNOWN
One of 86 stencils found
on the premises of a
decorator's suppliers in
Brussels. Stencil made
from cut card. Belgium,
about 1900–1920.
V&A: E.2914-1990

34
ERIC FORBES-
ROBERTSON
Drawing of a girl, seated,
reading a book that rests
on a tablet providing
space for a title, in a
landscape. Pencil on
paper. Britain, about 1902.
V&A: E.1988-1966

35
THOMAS STOTHARD
Study for composition
of groups, including
women with children
and a man on horseback.
Pencil drawing. England,
about 1815.
V&A: 9241:34

36
THOMAS STOTHARD
Sheet of studies of figures,
including women in
draped cloth and figures
in battle on horseback.
Pen and chalk drawing.
England, about 1815.
V&A: 9241:35

37
GEORGE
CRUIKSHANK
An envelope addressed
to G. Cruikshank Esq,
48 Mornington Place
that has been annotated
with text and sketches
including a view of man
in profile with top hat
smoking a pipe, and a
fairy with wings. Pencil,
pen and ink on paper.
Britain, 1850–78.
V&A: 9951P

38
FRANÇOIS-GÉDÉON
REVERDIN
Engraving depicting
four amorini or putti
dancing, holding a rope,
while a fifth beats a
drum. Geneva, early
19th century.
V&A: 17664

39
UNKNOWN
Drawing of five cherubic
child figures with needle
holes made through the
paper. Pen and ink on
paper. Europe, about 1874.
V&A: 26807:1

40
HENRY WILSON
One of 510 designs for
jewellery, silverwork and
jewellers' tools. Pencil,
pen and ink, chalk and
other media. Britain or
Italy, 1897–1912.
V&A: E.669:263-1955

41
UNKNOWN
Drawing of a dancing
bear with muzzle,
surrounded by three
men, one with a stick,
another with a club and
a third playing a horn.
Ink and watercolour
on paper. Europe,
18th–19th century.
V&A: 23694:23

42
REV. CHARLES
FREDERICK
GODBOLD TURNER
A drawing of the exterior
of a building. In a set
of 35 sheets, various
sizes. England, 1845–1918.
V&A: E.214-1919

43
UNKNOWN
Niello print depicting
the Nativity, above
are three angels, two
sounding trumpets and
the third holds a tablet
with *Gloria in excesis*.
Europe, before 1871.
V&A: 24771:1

44
UNKNOWN
Engraving depicting
Natura, the personifica-
tion of nature. She is
leaning towards a
reclining child while
expressing milk from
two of her six breasts.
The heads of a unicorn,
horse and lion are also
represented. Europe,
18th–19th century.
V&A: 27463:7

45
UNKNOWN
Engraving of a fluted
vase. *One foot ten inches and
a half* is printed along
the right side of the paper.
One of 329 prints of vases
grouped in a folio album.
Wood engraving on paper.
Britain, 19th century.
V&A: 28263:262

46
UNKNOWN
Drawing showing designs
for four carved chairs with
turned legs and open
backs. Pencil on paper.
Europe, 19th century.
V&A: 29486:100

47
UNKNOWN
Drawing showing a
seated figure in draped
cloth with helmet.
Pencil on paper.
V&A: 9955S

48
UNKNOWN
A print showing six
examples of ancient
metalwork, including
gold, brass, silver, shaped
into rings and labeled
'Ring Money'. Ink on paper.
Britain, 1857.
V&A: 29629:60

49
UNKNOWN
Print depicting an ancient
oil lamp with an image
of a menorah, on a
backdrop of a hanging
cloth. From a collection
of 893 printed scraps
and cuttings. Engraving
on paper. Europe,
18th–19th century.
V&A: 25016:700

50
LARRY RIVERS
Dark Camel drawing,
an interpretation of the
'Camel' cigarette packet.
Pencil and oil paint on
paper. USA, 1962.
V&A: CIRC.182-1964

51
UNKNOWN
A black and white
photograph of a young
man behind the wheel of
a convertible car. In the
foreground, projected on
to the door of the car,
is the shadow of the
photographer. USA,
mid 20th century.
*V&A: LOAN:AMERI-
CANFRIENDS.711:17-2016*

52
HENRY MOORE
Study of a reclining
nude. Pencil, black ink,
brown and yellow
washes. United
Kingdom, about 1930.
V&A: CIRC.10-1950

53
UNKNOWN
Drawing a seated
woman, surrounded
by four children; one
climbing on her back,
one breastfeeding, one
lying on her lap and the
other by her side. Sepia
ink on paper. Europe.
V&A: D.101-1885

54
UNKNOWN
A tinted sheet of paper
with nine studies in pen
of the Virgin and Child
and a large group. Pen
and ink wash. Europe,
before 1885.
V&A: D.103-1885

55
FRANCESCO
SIMONINI
Drawing, *A Melee of
Cavalry*. Pen and tint on
paper. Italy, 1689–1753.
V&A: D.108-1885

56
UNKNOWN
Tinted drawing of
Roman antiquities
and architecture,
one of 28. Pen on paper.
Italy, 18th century.
V&A: D.1023-1889

57
UNKNOWN
Fanciful decorative
design with Louis
Quatorze-style scrolls
and two birds. Pen and
ink drawing on a green
ground, on paper. Europe,
17th–18th century
V&A: D.364-1886

58
UNKNOWN
Design for a reliquary
or other receptacle with
a gridded window in
the middle. Pen and
wash drawing. Italy,
late 16th century.
V&A: D.323-1887

59
UNKNOWN
Tinted drawing of
Roman antiquities
and architecture, one
of 28. Pen on paper.
Italy, 18th century.
V&A: D.1030-1889

60
GIOVANNI BATTISTA
TIEPOLO
Sketches of cloaked figures.
Pen and wash, on paper.
Italy, about 1696–1770.
V&A: D.1825:190-1885

61
UNKNOWN
Drawing of *The Marriage
of the Blessed Virgin and
St Joseph*. Pen and wash
on paper.
V&A: D.1080-1900

62
PETER CAMPBELL
Illustration for the cover
of the *London Review of
Books*, 18 August 2005,
vol. 27, no. 16. Watercolour
on paper. England, 2005.
V&A: E.201-2020

63
UNKNOWN
Design for an elaborately
carved side table, with
draped female figures
forming the legs. From
a group of 42 designs,
on 21 sheets, for furniture.
Pencil on paper. England,
about 1870.
V&A: E.245-1955

64
HANS FEIBUSCH
A painting depicting three figures with a monkey in a circus fairground. One of 12 gouache designs for mural for the Tea Pavilion at the V&A's *Britain Can Make It* exhibition. Gouache on card. Britain, 1946.
V&A: E.139-1994

65
HANS FEIBUSCH
A painting depicting a circus caravan and booths, a carousel and a sculpture in a park, framed by a striped awning. 1 of 12 gouache designs for mural for the Tea Pavilion at the V&A's *Britain Can Make It* exhibition. Gouache on card. Britain, 1946.
V&A: E.138-1994

66
UNKNOWN
A drawing from a miscellaneous collection of 56 designs and studies, chiefly for silversmiths' work. Drawing on paper.
V&A: 9052:5

67
UNKNOWN
Design for a decoration for a ceiling.
V&A: 104

68
FRANCIS FRITH
Ruins of Martund. Cashmere. Part of the 'Universal Series' of topographical photographs. It depicts the ruins of the Surya temple in Kashmir. Whole-plate albumen print from wet collodion glass negative. 1850s to 1870s.
V&A: E.208:898-1994

69
FRANCIS FRITH
The Purana-Kila. Old Fort. Delhi. Part of the 'Universal Series' of topographical photographs. It depicts two circular towers and the gatehouse of the fort of Purana Qila, Delhi. Whole-plate albumen print from wet collodion glass negative. 1850s to 1870s.
V&A: E.208:1165-1994

70
LEOPOLD WILLIAM JONES
A drawing in watercolour, pen and pencil of a cut-glass candelabrum. The drawing is inscribed with the name of *Edmund Westby Esq.* England, 19th century.
V&A: E.27-1985

71
UNKNOWN
Drawing of the side of the Great Door of King's College, Cambridge. Pencil and pen and ink on paper. Britain, late 18th to mid 19th century.
V&A: E.215-2001

72
REV. CHARLES FREDERICK GODBOLD TURNER
Drawing of the exterior of a building. In a set of 35 sheets, various sizes. England, late 18th to early 19th century.
V&A: E.217-1919

73
ERIC GILL
Study of hands holding a cross, for the fifth Station of the Cross in Westminster Cathedral. 1 of 46 assorted studies. Pencil sketch on paper, 1913.
V&A: E.231-1924

74
ALEXANDER STRAHÜBER
(artist)
JOHANN JOCH
(engraver)
Print of *Esther and Haman*, from *The Art Journal*, 1854. Wood engraving.
V&A: E.1259:113-1886

75
UNKNOWN
Col Senno e con la Mano, engraved emblem from the book *The Royal Politician Represented in One Hundred Emblems*. Engraving on paper, cut out and pasted into a scrapbook. London, 1700.
V&A: E.254-1897

76
JÉRÔME DAVID
Print from a series entitled *Rembrandt's Heads*. Possibly Italy, mid 17th century.
V&A: E.1154-1885

77
PAUL NASH
Printed pattern design on newsprint, probably produced to check the registration between two print blocks. Britain, about 1930.
V&A: E.114-2021

78
HENDRICK GOLTZIUS
Quis Evadet. Print depicting an allegory of transience. Engraving on paper. Netherlands, 1594.
V&A: E.367-1887

79
CHRISTIANA GRACE TURNOUR GIBSON
Illustration depicting a chameleon. Probably copied from book illustrations. Watercolour on paper. Britain, 19th century.
V&A: E.425-1967

80
GODFREY SYKES
Design for the Royal Arms in the centre, surrounded by practice versions of motifs including lions and belt buckles. Pencil and pen and ink. England, mid-19th century.
V&A: E.467-2015

81
FREDERIC JAMES SHIELDS
Drawing of chandelier and part of a sofa in the Green Drawing Room, Windsor Castle. Pencil, pen and ink, wash and watercolour, heightened with white. England, 1874.
V&A: E.485-1951

82
WILLIAM DE MORGAN
Sketch design for a tile panel, *'BBB'*. Composed of large white flowers with purple centres. The central flower is unfinished. Watercolour and pencil on paper. Britain or Italy, about 1870–1907.
V&A: E.513-1917

83
MINNIE MCLEISH
One of 56 designs for textiles. Small, close design designed to give a subtle textured effect or rich surface. Pencil, ink, watercolour and bodycolour. Scotland, about 1935.
V&A: E.542:50-1971

84
UNKNOWN
Mother's Day card with an image of a mother holding her child. Germany, 20th century.
V&A: E.571-2008

85
MARTIN
ENGELBRECHT
One of 6 rectangular
cards with areas cut out,
depicting the interior
of an 18th century
artist's studio in 3D
when arranged in order
and viewed together.
Augsburg, Germany,
about 1740.
V&A: E.592:1 to 6-2009

86
WILLIAM DE MORGAN
Tile panel design
with fruiting branch.
Watercolour and pencil
on paper. Britain,
about 1870–88.
V&A: E.593-1917

87
KATHLEEN
SHEFFIELD
Design for dresses,
showing both popular
1840s and 1940s fashion.
Ink and paint on brown
paper. England, 1940.
V&A: E.603-2015

88
WILLIAM DE MORGAN
Tile panel design
with fruiting branch.
Watercolour and pencil.
England or Italy, 1886–88.
V&A: E.629-1917

89
MARIA LUIZA AMARAL
Perspective view of the
interior of a Murphy
Radio, created during
the artist's wartime
service as a technical
illustrator. Pencil, pen
and ink drawing.
Britain, about 1942.
V&A: E.646-1985

90
UNKNOWN
Stencil made from cut
card, one of 86 found
on the premises of a
decorators' suppliers
in Brussels. Belgium,
about 1900–20.
V&A: E.2900-1990

91
ERIC FORBES-
ROBERTSON
Nude figures embracing,
pencil drawing.
Britain, late 19th to
early 20th century.
V&A: E.1934-1966

92
ERIC FORBES-
ROBERTSON
Study of a dog,
illustration to the
children's story
Revolution by Frances
Forbes-Robertson.
Pencil drawing.
Britain, late 19th to
early 20th century.
V&A: E.2016-1966

93
ERIC FORBES-
ROBERTSON
One of two drawings
for an illustration.
Pencil, Indian ink and
chinese white on tracing
paper. Britain or France,
about 1885–1935.
V&A: E.2102-1966

94
WILLIAM DE MORGAN
Design for a square
tile, with formal
flowers and leaves in
blue. Watercolour
and pencil on paper.
Britain, 1870–88.
V&A: E.768-1917

95
LOUISA STUART
Drawing of a dog,
from an album of loose
drawings and sketches.
Pen and sepia ink drawing.
Britain, 1833–39.
V&A: E.840-1987

96
DUNCAN GRANT
Textile design for
Allan Walton Textiles.
Watercolour and pencil,
some collage. Britain,
mid 20th century.
V&A: E.845-1978

97
WILLIAM DE MORGAN
Tile design with
winged creatures,
pricked for transfer.
Watercolour and pencil
on paper. Britain, 1870–88.
V&A: E.906-1917

98
JAMES GILLRAY
Print depicting *The King
of Brobdingnag and Gulliver*.
A hand-coloured etching.
England 1800–1900.
V&A: 23685:15

99
BERNARD LEACH
Design for two biscuit
barrels. Pencil drawing.
Britain, 1940–50.
V&A: E.1210-1978

100
WILLIAM DE MORGAN
Design for a square tile
depicting a confrontation
between a snake and a
rabbit. Sepia watercolour
and pencil on paper.
Britain, 1872–88
V&A: E.958-1917

101
UNKNOWN
Design for a canopied
bed, draped in fabric
with red floral motifs.
Watercolour drawing
on paper. France, early
19th century.
V&A: E.978-1921

102
G. STEINLE
(artist)
JOHANN JOCH
(engraver)
Print depicting *Paul
preaching at Antioch*.
Wood engraving.
Germany, 19th century.
V&A: E.1259:117-1886

103
UNKNOWN
ENGRAVER
after
ALBRECHT DÜRER
Printed cutting
depicting St Anne, her
hands clasped together.
Based on an image by
Dürer. One of 372 assorted
prints from a scrapbook,
mainly taken from
1100s–1400s manuscripts.
Britain, mid 19th century.
V&A: E.1260:211-1886

104
WILLIAM DE MORGAN
Three border designs
for circular dishes,
decorated with fruiting
and flowering foliage
and grotesque birds.
Parts of the designs are
pricked for transfer. Pencil
and sepia wash. England,
late 19th century.
V&A: E.1284-1917

105
AMBROSE MCEVOY
Portrait of a woman in a
hat. Ink and watercolour.
Britain, early 20th century.
V&A: E.1295-1935

106
SOMERS CLARKE
Measured sketches
of details (including
windows, arcadings, and
mouldings) of a cathedral.
Pencil drawing on paper.
England, 1866.
V&A: E.2770-1909

107
WILLIAM DE MORGAN
Persian flower and
leaf motifs for ceramic
decoration. Pencil and
watercolour. England,
late 19th century.
V&A: E.1437-1917

108
WILLIAM DE MORGAN
Three vase designs,
with floral band, leaping
lion and procession of deer.
Pencil and wash. England,
late 19th century.
V&A: E.1349-1917

109
AMBROSE MCEVOY
Study of a seated woman.
Pencil and Indian ink
on paper. Britain, early
20th century.
V&A: E.1300-1935

110
UNKNOWN
Army Navy Law Church,
drawing with four
caricatured figures.
Pen and ink and
watercolour on paper.
Britain, 18th –19th
century.
V&A: 23694:30

111
GEORGE
CRUIKSHANK
Study of hands
holding a glass, one
finger outstretched.
Pen and wash on paper.
Britain, before 1845.
V&A: 9998B

112
WILLIAM DE MORGAN
Vase design with
deer. Sepia and blue
wash on paper. England,
late 19th century.
V&A: E.1355-1917

113
WILLIAM DE MORGAN
Motifs of grotesque
creatures for ceramic
decoration. Sepia wash
on paper. England,
late 19th century.
V&A: E.1400-1917

114
E. LEVASSEUR
Design for a wooden
chair. Pencil, pen and
ink and watercolour on
paper. England, 1891–1908.
V&A: E.1332-1966

115
JOHN UPTON
Design of butterflies and
flowers, probably for the
lavatory of the Lion and
Unicorn public house,
Brighton. Felt tip pen
and collage. About 1975.
V&A: E.1818-1977

116
WILLIAM DE MORGAN
Leaf and animal motifs
for ceramic decoration.
The designs are pricked
for transfer. Sepia wash
on paper. England, late
19th century.
V&A: E.1489-1917

117
UNKNOWN
Vase with satyr and
goat. Hand-coloured
print. Possibly 1820.
V&A: E.1527A/180-1885

118
E. LEVASSEUR
Pencil drawing of
ornament. Drawing
in pencil, pen and ink,
wash and watercolour.
England, 1891–1908.
V&A: E.1519-1966

119
UNKNOWN
Sheet of designs for
chair back and sash
handles. Lettered with
title, stock numbers,
measurement and prices.
Lithograph on paper.
Britain, late 19th to
early 20th century.
V&A: E.1529-1966

120
UNKNOWN
Advertisement for
an unnamed chair
manufacturer, depicting
a room filled with
upholstered chairs.
Wood engraving on
paper. Britain, late 19th
to early 20th century.
V&A: E.1533-1966

121
UNKNOWN
Advertisement for an
unnamed furniture
manufacturer, with
a selection of heavily
upholstered chairs,
sofas and ottomans.
Wood engraving on
paper. Britain, late 19th
to early 20th century.
V&A: E.1537-1966

122
UNKNOWN
Drawing showing a
view of the Jacobean
manor house at Caradoc.
Watercolour on paper.
Britain, late 19th century.
V&A: E.1579:218-1885

123
WILLIAM DE MORGAN
Section drawings showing
the design of a kiln for
firing ceramics. Pencil
and watercolour drawing
on paper. Britain, late
19th century.
V&A: E.1625-1917

124
UNKNOWN
Design for transfer-
printed decoration
on ceramics, probably
a large circular dish.
Flowers and lace patterns.
Pen and ink drawing
on paper. Britain,
about 1820–80.
V&A: E.1733-1973

125
WILLIAM HARRY
ROGERS
Design for a strapwork
pattern. Pen and wash
over preliminary pencil
drawing on paper.
Britain, 1850–73.
V&A: E.1663-1979

126
UNKNOWN
Advertisement for
an unnamed furniture
manufacturer, depicting
a furniture unit with
integrated seating,
dresser and shelving.
Wood engraving on
paper. Britain, late 19th
to early 20th century.
V&A: E.1587-1966

127
ERIC FORBES-
ROBERTSON
Sketch of a woodcutter
climbing a tree. Pen and
ink drawing. Britain, 1877.
V&A: E.1805-1966

128
ERIC FORBES-
ROBERTSON
Drawing of a comic
actor on stage, dancing.
Drawing in pencil,
pen and ink and
watercolour on paper.
Britain, about 1875–80.
V&A: E.1809-1966

129
STEFANO DELLA
BELLA
Print depicting a ship
with an elaborately
decorated stern.
Etching on paper.
Italy, about 1645.
V&A: E.1866-1889

130
MICHELANGELO
PERGOLISI
One of 65 plates of
designs for arabesques
and other ornaments.
Etching. England, 1777.
V&A: 19541:6

131
ERIC FORBES-
ROBERTSON
E. Holman Clark as
Captain Hook in a
production of J.M. Barrie's
Peter Pan. Drawing in black
chalk. England, 1910.
V&A: E.1977-1966

132
UNKNOWN
Design for textile or fabric,
with blue, pink, red and
white flowers and foliage.
Pen and ink and watercol-
our drawing on paper.
France, late 18th–early
19th century.
V&A: E.4066-1911

133
ERIC FORBES-
ROBERTSON
Pencil sketch of a nude
woman, seen from behind.
Pencil drawing on paper.
Britain, 1865–1935.
V&A: E.2156-1966

134
ERIC FORBES-
ROBERTSON
Print in black ink of a
stylised flower, with a
line above and abstract
border below. Woodcut
on paper. Scotland, 1894.
V&A: E.2199-1966

135
UNKNOWN
Drawing of seven
stringed instruments,
annotated with titles
in Latin. Pen and ink
drawing on paper.
Europe.
V&A: E.2624-1886

136
After RAPHAEL
Print of the figure of
Poetry, after a fresco
by Raphael. Printed
ink on paper.
V&A: E.2681-1886

137
UNKNOWN
Printed cutting of two
amorini. Engraving,
cut and pasted on to
paper. Europe, 18th–
19th century.
V&A: E.2654-1886

138
UNKNOWN
Drawing of the waterfall
at the Powerscourt
Estate, Enniskerry.
Pen and ink and wash
drawing on paper. Ireland,
first half 19th century.
V&A: E.1319-1924

139
UNKNOWN
Architectural drawing
split into two designs.
Tinted pen drawing.
Netherlands.
V&A: D.1834-1885

140
EDNA CLARKE HALL
Study of a boy, three
quarter length. Red
chalk, pencil and
watercolour drawing
on paper. England, 1912.
V&A: E.2923-1948

141
CRETI DONATO
Designs for an *Adoration
of the Magi* and *Adoration of
the Shepherds* and studies
for the *Virgin and Child*.
Pen and ink on paper.
Italy, 1690.
V&A: E.3268-1948

142
ERIC FORBES-
ROBERTSON
Design for the title-page
of a magazine called *Les
Livres*. Drawing in pencil,
pen and ink and blue
crayon. Britain, late 19th–
early 20th century.
V&A: E.1913-1966

143
UNKNOWN
Sepia-coloured
photograph of Emperor
Napoleon III, the
Empress Eugénie and
the Prince Imperial Louis
Napoleon. France, 1860s.
V&A: 1210-1939

144
ERIC FORBES-
ROBERTSON
The Verdict, drawing of
a woman in classical
costume, seated on the
edge of a stage. One of 11
designs for head-pieces
for *Revue Française illustrée*.
Drawing in pencil and
pen and ink, on paper.
France, 1892.
V&A: E.1854-1966

145
UNKNOWN
Printed image cut
from *The Illustrated
London News*, depicting
a silver-gilt cup.
Wood engraving on
paper. England, 1856.
V&A: E.5222-1900

146
ERIC FORBES-
ROBERTSON
Illustration of the Devil
for *The Devil's Pronoun and
other Phantasies*. Drawing
in pencil and India ink
on paper. England, 1893.
V&A: E.1865-1966

147
JACQUES BELLANGE
Print depicting three
women, two with haloes
and one holding a palm
leaf. Etching and stipple on
paper. France, about 1610.
V&A: F.141:3

148
ERIC FORBES-
ROBERTSON
One of two drawings for
an illustration depicting a
man and woman looking
down at a woman, who is
addressing a young girl.
Drawing in pencil, Indian
ink and chinese white on
tracing paper. Britain or
France, about 1885–1935.
V&A: E.2103-1966

149
ERIC FORBES-
ROBERTSON
Sketch for an advertise-
ment for OXO, showing
a front view of a bull.
Drawing in Indian ink
and blue crayon on paper.
Britain or France,
1885–1935.
V&A: E.2134-1966

150
GIOVANNI
FRANCESCO CRESCI
(artist)
ANDREA MARELLI
(engraver)
Letter Q in a strapwork
border with a standing,
pointing putto and
various birds on either
side. From *Il Perfetto
Scrittore*. Engraving.
Italy, 1570.
V&A: E.2725-1910

First published in 2022 by CentreCentre
in association with V&A Publishing.

CentreCentre
215a Kingsland Road
London E2 8AN
hello@centrecentre.co.uk
www.centrecentre.co.uk

ISBN 978-1-9164121-7-0

Collected and photographed by George Eksts
Designed and edited by Patrick Fry Studio
Copy editing by Emily Watkins
Printed by Gomer, Wales

British Library Cataloguing-in-Publication Data.
A catalogue record for this book is available from
the British Library.

V&A Publishing

Supporting the world's leading
museum of art and design,
the Victoria and Albert
Museum, London